METRIC MATH

BY ERIN ASH SULLIVAN

TABLE OF CONTENTS

INTRODUCTION

People have been using measurements for thousands of years. A measurement is a number followed by a unit. Temperature, size, and distance are among the many things that can be described by a measurement.

You use measurements every day to explore and describe the world around you. You go to a doctor's office and monitor your height and weight. You use a meat thermometer to cook your foods to the desired doneness. You tell a friend how far your home is from school. You read a weather map to learn the day's temperature, humidity, and wind speed.

Many early units of measure were based on the human body. Ancient Egyptians measured length with a cubit—the distance between the elbow and the middle finger. Ancient Greeks measured height in hands. Each hand was the width of the four fingers on one hand.

SOLVE THIS! 1

A "hand" equals about 4 inches. Use this information to solve the following problems.

a. How many inches tall at its shoulder is a 15-hand horse? How many feet is this?

b. How many hands tall is a 96-inch wall? A 12-foot wall?

c. How many hands tall is a 1-foot dog?

These systems were not very accurate. Do you know why? Compare the length of a cubit on your arm to the length of a cubit on an adult's arm. An adult's cubit is probably longer than yours. So the measurements you and an adult would make would be different! Measurements don't mean much without a **standard unit**. A standard unit has a fixed value. It is exactly the same wherever you go.

Today, people measure with standard units. An inch is a standard unit used to measure length. An inch is a standard unit in the **Imperial system**, or English system, of measurement. The Imperial system was once used around the world. Today, it is used mainly in the United States.

SOLVE THIS! 2

Joseph Louis LaGrange helped to create the metric system in France in 1790. How many years ago was that?

About two hundred years ago, the **metric system** of measurement was created. The metric system is a decimal system. That means it is based on the number 10.

In 1875, 18 countries signed the Treaty of the Meter and adopted the metric system. The United States continues to use the Imperial system.

All units in the metric system are divided into 10 equal parts. Because 10 is an easy number to multiply by or divide by, the metric system is easy to use. It has become common around the world.

In this book, you will learn about four basic measurements—length, mass, volume, and temperature. You will also learn which metric system units are used to measure them.

LENGTH

You measure **length** when you find the distance between two points. People measure length for many reasons. A person making a kite will measure the length of string needed. A pilot will measure the distance between cities. A doctor will keep track of a patient's growth by regularly measuring his or her height, or the distance from head to feet.

The basic unit of length in the metric system is the **meter (m)**. One meter is about the same length as 3 feet, or an Imperial yard.

It's a FACT!

The measurements we call height, width, and distance are all measurements of length.

Height is a measurement of length.

The Nile River is about 6,650,000 meters long!
The average ladybug is between 0.004
(⁴/₁,₀₀₀) and 0.008 (⁸/₁,₀₀₀) meter long!

The meter is not a practical unit for measuring all lengths. Sometimes a smaller unit is needed. For example, you would not want to measure the length of a ladybug in meters. Sometimes a unit larger than a meter is needed. The length of the Nile River in Africa would be very hard to measure in meters. For this reason, other units based on the meter were developed.

These units are related to the meter by multiples of 10. That means they are 10 times larger or smaller, 100 times larger or smaller, 1,000 times larger or smaller, and so forth.

If a meter is divided into 10 equal parts, each smaller part, or unit, is called a decimeter (dm). This means one decimeter is 1/10 of a meter. A decimeter, in turn, can be divided into 10 equal parts. These units are called centimeters (cm). One centimeter is 1/10 of a decimeter and 1/100 of a meter. A centimeter can be divided into 10 millimeters (mm). One millimeter is 1/1,000 of a meter. These smaller units can be used to measure lengths too short to be measured in meters.

To measure longer lengths, such as the length of the Nile River, the kilometer (km) is used. There are 1,000 meters in a kilometer.

SOLVE THIS! 3

Use the information on the chart to solve the following problems.
a. How many centimeters are in 5 meters?
b. How many millimeters are in 3 decimeters?
c. How many decimeters are in 2 meters?
d. How many meters are in 2 kilometers?
e. Which is larger, 1,000 millimeters or 1 meter?

10 decimeters	= 1 meter
10 centimeters	= 1 decimeter
100 centimeters	= 1 meter
10 millimeters	= 1 centimeter
1,000 millimeters	= 1 meter
1,000 meters	= 1 kilometer

The most common tool for measuring length in the metric system is a meterstick. To measure the length of an object with a curved edge, such as the distance around your waist, you would use a tape measure. A tape measure is more flexible.

SOLVE THIS! 4

Which tool and unit would be best for finding the following:

a. the length of a classroom wall?
b. the distance around your wrist?
c. the height of a flagpole?

9

MASS

Look for the scale in this painting. Ancient Egyptians believed that the gods measured the souls of the dead to see if they had done good deeds in life.

Mass is another property used to describe things around us. Mass tells us how much of something there is. For example, when you tell a grocery clerk how much fruit or meat you want, you are describing mass. Mass is a measure of the amount of material an object has.

People often use the word **weight** when they are really describing mass. Mass and weight are related, but they are not the same. The relationship between mass and weight can seem tricky!

Weight is a measure of the pull of **gravity** on an object. Gravity is a force that pulls objects toward each other. Your weight describes the pull of Earth's gravity on you. The more mass an object has, the more it will weigh.

If you were to travel to the Moon, you would find that you weigh less there than you do on Earth. Gravity is weaker on the Moon because the Moon has less mass than Earth. However, your mass would not change. The amount of material that makes up you or any object remains the same no matter where the object is.

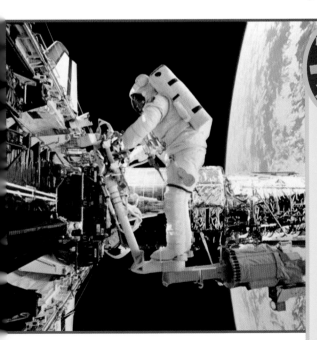

The pull of gravity is almost zero when astronauts orbit Earth. Although these astronauts are practically weightless, their masses have not changed.

SOLVE THIS! 5

The pull of gravity on the Moon is about 1/6 the pull on Earth. Use a calculator to find the Moon weights of the objects below.
a. a cat that weighs 12 pounds on Earth
b. an Asian elephant that weighs 10,000 pounds on Earth

The basic unit of mass in the metric system is the **kilogram (kg)**. One kilogram has a mass of about 2.2 pounds. Pounds are units in the Imperial system.

The kilogram is used to measure the mass of large objects. For example, you would measure the mass of a car in kilograms. To measure the mass of small objects, you would use the gram (g). Grams are used to measure amounts listed on food containers. To measure the mass of even smaller objects, you would use the milligram (mg). The mass of a sheet of paper would be measured in milligrams.

There are 1,000 grams in a kilogram. There are 1,000 milligrams in a gram. How many milligrams are in a kilogram?

What unit of mass would you use to measure the sumo wrestler? What unit of mass would you use to measure the mouse?

People use **scales** to measure mass. There are many different kinds of scales. Each is designed for a different use. Some, such as the triple beam balance, are very accurate and good for scientific experiments. Others, such as a produce scale, are less accurate but handy for quick measurements.

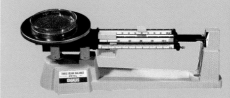
triple beam balance

produce scale

SOLVE THIS!
6

What was the shopper's total bill for fruit?

1.5 (1 ½) kg apples at $2.00 per kg
3.0 kg oranges at $1.50 per kg
2.0 kg bananas at $1.75 per kg

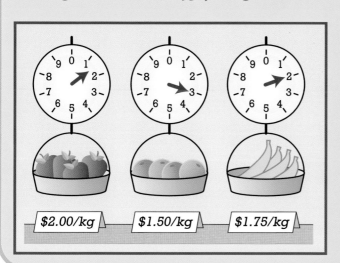

$2.00/kg $1.50/kg $1.75/kg

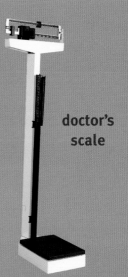
doctor's scale

VOLUME

The amount of space an object takes up is called its **volume**. People measure volume when they follow a recipe or fill the gas tank of their car. You keep track of volume when you pour a glass of orange juice. You do this by estimating how much juice will fill your glass. If you don't estimate correctly, you're in for a spill!

SOLVE THIS! 7

Use the chart below to answer the questions.

8 ounces	=	1 cup
2 cups	=	1 pint
2 pints	=	1 quart
4 quarts	=	1 gallon

a. How many cups are in a quart?
b. How many pints are in a gallon?
c. How many cups are in a gallon?
d. How many ounces are in 3 cups?

Cups, pints, quarts, and gallons are units used to measure volume in the Imperial system. If you look around your kitchen, you will probably see many containers whose volumes are given in these units.

The basic unit of volume in the metric system is the **liter (L)**. A liter is a little more than a quart. To measure volumes smaller than a liter, you would use the milliliter (mL). There are 1,000 milliliters in a liter.

An ordinary drinking glass holds about 200 milliliters of liquid. Some cartons of milk hold about one liter of liquid. A large bottle of soda holds 2 liters of liquid.

These three containers have very different shapes. However, they all hold the same volume of liquid.

To measure very large volumes of liquids, the kiloliter (kL) is used. A kiloliter is 1,000 liters.

People measure the volume of liquids with measuring cups, measuring spoons, beakers, and graduated cylinders. These tools have marks that tell how much liquid is in the container.

 SOLVE THIS! 8

Which metric unit of volume would be used to measure the following:
a. the amount of cough syrup a person should take at one time?
b. the amount of orange juice to get for four people?
c. the amount of gasoline to fill up a car's tank?

 9

Which is a better bargain: a half liter of water for $0.79 or two liters for $2.50? Explain how you got your answer.

Liters and milliliters are the metric units used to measure the volumes of liquids. To measure the volume of a solid, the metric unit used is the cubic centimeter (cc). One cubic centimeter is equal to one milliliter.

The volume of some solids, such as books and boxes, can be determined by multiplying the solid's height times its length times its width. The volume of solids that do not have regular shapes cannot be determined this way. Rocks and sticks are examples of solids that do not have regular shapes. To measure the volume of these solids, a method called **displacement** is used.

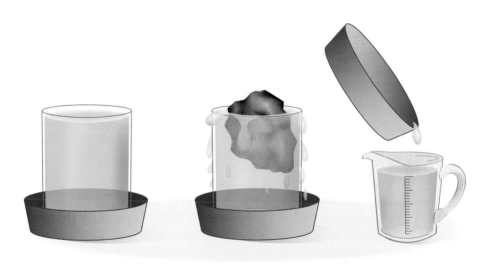

In the displacement method for measuring volume, a container is filled with a known amount of water. When the solid is placed in the container, water will be displaced and will overflow the container. The volume of water displaced is equal to the volume of the solid.

TEMPERATURE

Temperature describes how hot or cold an object is. When you think about temperature, you probably think of the weather. Temperature is a very important factor of weather. However, the temperatures of many other things are measured all the time. For example, people measure their body temperature to check their health. Cooks keep track of the temperature in their ovens when they bake. Scientists measure the temperature of reactions they do in the laboratory.

F-2° DIV.   C-1°DIV.

230 110
220 100
210
200 90
190
180 80
170
160 70
150
140 60
130
120 50
110
100 40
90
80 30
70
60 20
50
40
30 10
20
10
0
10
20
30

SOLVE THIS! 10

The hottest planet in our solar system is Venus, with an average temperature of 449°C. The coldest is Pluto, with an average temperature of −234°C. What is the range (difference) of temperatures between the two?

You can find thermostats in ovens and attached to heating systems. Thermostats set a target temperature and turn the heat on or off in order to stay on target.

Vostok, Antarctica, is the coldest place on Earth. The coldest temperature ever recorded there was −89°C.

El Azizia, Libya, is the hottest place on Earth with a record temperature of 57.2°C.

SOLVE THIS! 11

This table shows high temperatures for one week in April in Los Angeles. Use the data to create a bar graph. Then find the following:
a. the maximum
b. the minimum
c. the range
d. the average

Monday	20°C
Tuesday	22°C
Wednesday	19°C
Thursday	21°C
Friday	26°C
Saturday	27°C
Sunday	28°C

In the metric system, temperature is measured on the **Celsius** (SEHL-see-uhs) **(C)** scale. This scale is based on the freezing and boiling points of water. Water freezes at 0°C. Water boils at 100°C. There are exactly 100 degrees between the freezing point and boiling point of water.

On the Celsius scale, normal body temperature of humans is 37°. Comfortable room temperature is 21°.

The tool used for measuring temperature is the **thermometer**. A thermometer is a long, thin tube filled with liquid. As the liquid gets warmer, it expands and rises in the tube. The opposite happens as the liquid gets cooler. It contracts, or shrinks, and drops in the tube.

Early thermometers were filled with mercury. Today, many thermometers are filled with colored alcohol. Many of the newest thermometers give a digital readout.

 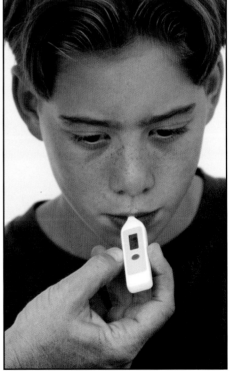

Traditional thermometers contain liquids that expand as they get warmer. Modern thermometers use electronic devices.

 **Point**

Make Connections

You can make measurements similar to those made by mathematicians and scientists all over the world by using the same metric "language"!

Here are some measurements about yourself and your surroundings for you to make. Use the metric units of length, mass, volume, and temperature that you have learned. Create a chart to record your findings.

- outdoor temperature

- your height

- your mass

- distance to school

- foot length

- volume of water you drink at each meal

- mass of your favorite toy

- volume of water in your neighborhood pool

1 page 3:
a. 60 inches, 5 feet; b. 24 hands, 36 hands; c. 3 hands

2 page 4:
213 years in 2003

3 page 8:
a. 500 cm; b. 300 mm; c. 20 dm; d. 2,000 meters;
e. they are the same

4 page 9:
 a. meterstick, meter; b. tape measure,
centimeter; c. meterstick, meter

5 page 11:
a. 2 pounds; b. 1666.667 pounds

6 page 13:
$11.00; $3.00 for apples + $4.50 for oranges
+ $3.50 for bananas

7 page 14:
a. 4 cups; b. 8 pints; c. 16 cups; d. 24 ounces

8 page 16:
milliliter; liter; liter

9 page 16:
Two liters for $2.50 is the better buy.
Four half-liters equal 2 liters. That would cost $3.16.

10 page 18:
683°C

11 page 19:
a. maximum is 28°; b. minimum is 19°; c. range is 9°;
d. average is 23.29°

GLOSSARY

Celsius (C)	(SEHL-see-uhs) the temperature scale used in the metric system (page 19)
displacement	(dihs-PLAYS-ment) the method of measuring the volume of an irregular solid by finding out how much water it moves out of the way (page 17)
gravity	(GRAV-ih-tee) a force that pulls objects toward each other (page 11)
Imperial system	(ihm-PEER-ee-ul SIHS-tuhm) the system of measurement established in Europe during the Middle Ages (page 4)
kilogram (kg)	(KIHL-uh-gram) the basic unit of mass in the metric system (page 12)
length	(LAYNGTH) the distance between two points (page 6)
liter (L)	(LEE-ter) the basic unit of volume in the metric system (page 15)
mass	(MAS) the amount of material in an object (page 10)
meter (m)	(MEE-ter) the basic unit of length in the metric system (page 6)
metric system	(MEH-trihk SIHS-tuhm) the system of measurement developed about 200 years ago (page 4)
scale	(SKAYL) tool for measuring weight (page 13)
standard unit	(STAND-erd YOON-iht) a unit that has a fixed value (page 4)
temperature	(TEMP-er-uh-cher) the measure of hot or cold (page 18)
thermometer	(ther-MAHM-ih-ter) a tool for measuring temperature (page 20)
volume	(VAHL-yoom) the amount of space an object takes up (page 14)
weight	(WAYT) the measure of gravity's pull on an object (page 10)

INDEX